WILD ABO

GREAT WHITE SHARKS

By Martha London

Kaleidoscope
Minneapolis, MN

Bigfoot Books

The Quest for Discovery Never Ends

....

This edition first published in 2020 by Kaleidoscope Publishing, Inc.

No part of this publication may be reproduced in whole or in part without written permission of the publisher.

For information regarding permission, write to
Kaleidoscope Publishing, Inc.
6012 Blue Circle Drive
Minnetonka, MN 55343

Library of Congress Control Number
2019938852

ISBN
978-1-64519-006-6 (library bound)
978-1-64494-248-2 (paperback)
978-1-64519-106-3 (ebook)

Text copyright © 2020 by Kaleidoscope Publishing, Inc. All-Star Sports, Bigfoot Books, and associated logos are trademarks and/or registered trademarks of Kaleidoscope Publishing, Inc.

Printed in the United States of America.

FIND ME IF YOU CAN!

Bigfoot lurks within one of the images in this book. It's up to you to find him!

TABLE OF CONTENTS

Chapter 1: Powerful Predator *4*

Chapter 2: Ruler of the Sea *10*

Chapter 3: Home Is Where the Tail Rests *16*

Chapter 4: Saving Sharks *22*

    Beyond the Book... *28*
    Research Ninja.. *29*
    Further Resources.. *30*
    Glossary *31*
    Index *32*
    Photo Credits.. *32*
    About the Author... *32*

CHAPTER 1

Powerful Predator

A great white shark swims in the ocean. She is near the coast of South Africa. The sun is high in the sky. The water is clear and calm. She swims slowly. Sharks don't need to be in a hurry. She's 16 feet (4.9 m) long. The shark knows seals will come along. They hang out along the sandy coast.

The shark uses her sharp eyesight to watch the surface. Her sensitive nose smells a seal. She heads toward the scent. The shark dives deeper. She doesn't want to scare the seal away.

Great white sharks are found in oceans all over the world.

Great white sharks are excellent hunters.

The seal is looking for a meal, too. It's hunting for fish in the ocean. It doesn't see the shark below.

The seal passes above. The shark takes aim. She gathers speed. The shark explodes through the surface. When she **breaches**, the seal is caught between her jaws. Her sharp teeth tear the seal's body. Sharks don't chew their food. She swallows each piece whole.

FUN FACT
Great white sharks can smell one drop of blood in 25 gallons (95 L) of water.

The smell of blood brings more sharks. If any pieces are left, the other great whites will clean up. The big great white swims away. She disappears into the blue water.

Home is the whole ocean. Dinner is whatever sits on the surface. She lives by herself. She doesn't like groups.

Great white sharks are solitary creatures.

She'll stay in these waters for a few months. But great white sharks like to **roam**. In a few months, she'll swim toward Australia. She'll cross 6,800 miles (11,000 km). She'll spend some time around Western Australia. Then she'll swim back to South Africa.

CHAPTER 2

Ruler of the Sea

This shark's mother gave birth to him in warm water. He's already more than 3 feet (.9 m) long. The shark was born with many siblings. But they left after they were born. The shark's mother doesn't stick around. She doesn't need to. Even a young great white can take care of himself.

He follows the same **migration** patterns as his mother. The shark doesn't learn these skills. He knows them when he's born. He swims from California to the middle of the Pacific Ocean. The water turns colder. The shark dives down to find food. He can dive more than 1,500 feet (460 m). It's dark that far down. But the shark has a great sense of smell.

FUN FACT
Unlike most fish, great white sharks are born live rather than hatched.

Young great white sharks live on their own.

The young shark grows slowly. It will take twenty years before he is fully grown. By then, he'll be more than 12 feet (3.7 m) long. He'll weigh more than 2,000 pounds (900 kg). He won't be as big as the females. But he'll still be able to eat whatever he wants. For now, he eats fish and squid.

The name "great white" comes from their white underbelly.

PARTS OF A SHARK

powerful nose that can smell a single drop of blood

dorsal fin

sharp, serrated teeth

gills for breathing

strong tail

As the shark grows, he expands his **territory**. The shark is **endothermic**. Unlike most sharks, great whites can control their body temperature. The shark can explore cold waters. He might even roam as far north as Alaska. But he always comes back to the California waters. He was born here. This is his home base. There is a large population of seals. This makes finding a meal easy.

Seals are a common meal for sharks.

CHAPTER 3

Home Is Where the Tail Rests

Great white sharks live around the world. Their populations aren't large. But they live in waters near every continent except Antarctica.

This great white shark is exploring. The shark swims near the coast of the northeastern United States.

FUN FACT
Great white females are larger than males.

Great whites are the largest predatory sharks.

She arrives around June. She stays near Massachusetts for the summer.

Her tail never rests for very long. She moves up and down the coast. In October, she'll wander south to warmer water.

Where Do Great White Sharks Live?

Climate change has made the water warmer near Massachusetts. She doesn't mind. She can always spend more time up north. But only if there's food. And only if there isn't competition. Other sharks like the warmer water, too. More of them stay up here for longer periods of time. This shark is pretty shy. She doesn't like fighting over space. She'd rather look for a meal somewhere else.

TRACKING GREAT WHITES

Scientists learn a lot about sharks by tracking them. They attach trackers to a shark's dorsal fin. Scientists tracked a great white named Lydia. She traveled more than 20,000 miles (32,000 km). Scientists didn't know sharks could swim that far. Lydia swam farther than any other shark they had tracked.

Great white sharks breach to hunt.

She starts migrating toward Florida. Light shines off the top of the water. The shark swims slowly below. She can dive for fish. But she usually watches the surface. The shark likes hunting for food above her. It's easier to surprise her **prey**.

Her big hunting grounds up north have seals. The seals have a lot of fat. They give the shark more energy.

Sharks are easily spotted by their dorsal fins.

FUN FACT
A great white's tooth can be up to 6.6 inches (16.8 cm) long!

As she moves south, seal isn't always on the menu. There are a lot of birds and fish. Sometimes she'll find whales that are already dead.

The shark spends the winter in Florida. She cruises near the southern tip of the state. In May, she begins her journey toward Massachusetts again.

CHAPTER 4

Saving Sharks

A great white is swimming near Australia. There are beaches here. The water is warm. It's a sunny day. Beams of light hit the shark's back. He sees some commotion closer to shore. The shark wants to check it out. He's curious about what's going on.

As he gets closer, there is a strange shape in the water. He doesn't know what it is. His mouth is the best way to figure it out. He uses his teeth to bite down on a long thing. It's an **exploratory** bite. Suddenly there is a lot of splashing and screaming. Something hits his nose. But he already let go. He doesn't like the taste of people. The shark swims away.

Beaches have signs warning people if sharks have been sighted.

Movies and TV shows can make some people afraid of sharks. They show violent shark attacks. A shark sneaks up on a person. It drags the person away. The water is red. People scream. But people aren't a shark's first choice for food.

Shark populations are **vulnerable**. Great whites are shy. They are hard to find. Scientists spend many hours trying to track the sharks down. Sometimes they dive with sharks. It is important to study great whites. Diving with sharks helps scientists understand their temperament.

Fishermen throw **gill nets** into the ocean to catch fish. Sometimes great whites get tangled in the nets. Sharks need to swim to breathe. The gill nets trap them. They can't swim.

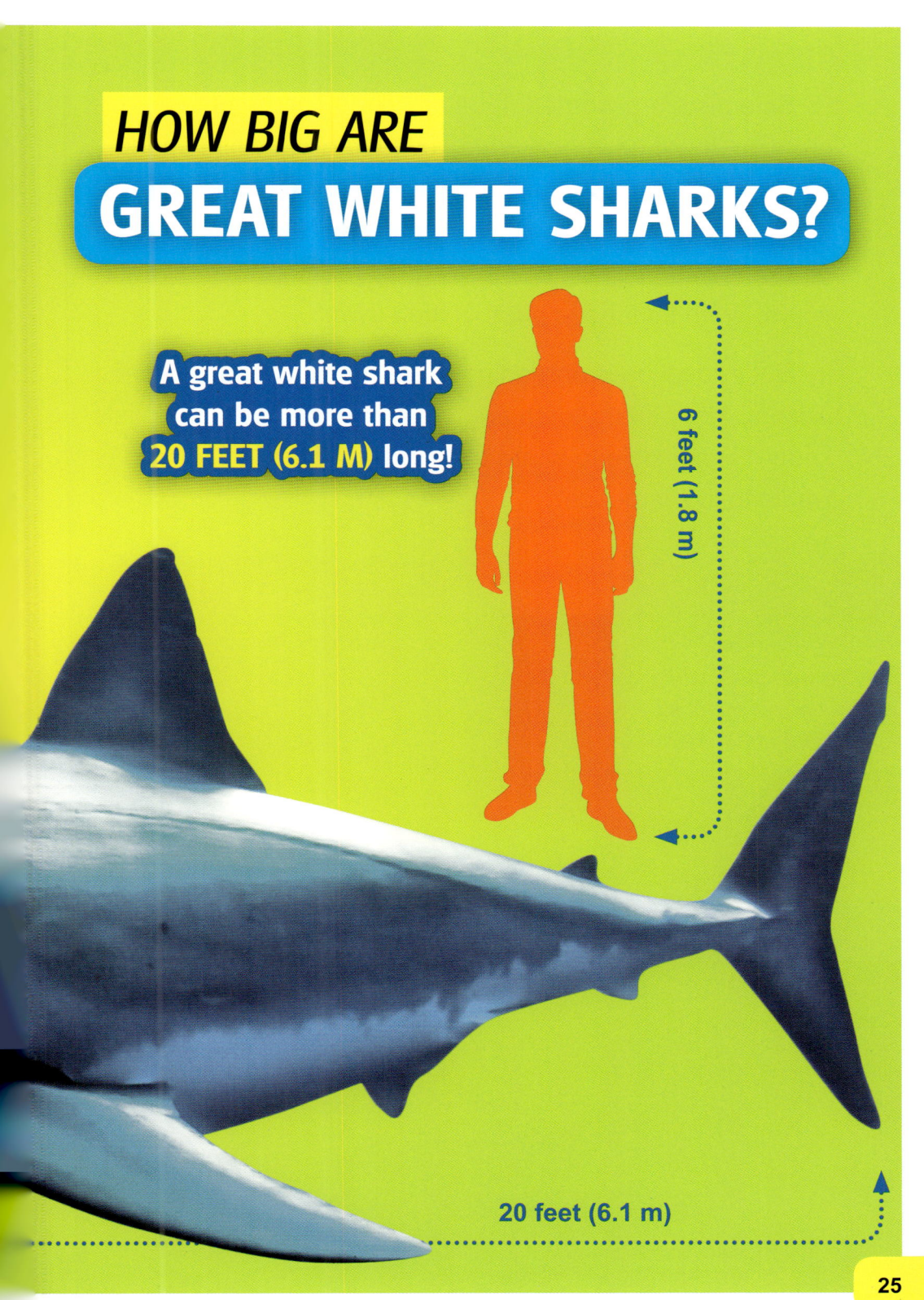

Scientists are worried. It takes a long time for sharks to grow up. It will be very hard to save the great white shark population. A female shark only gives birth every two years. She takes a long break between pregnancies. She travels far out into the ocean. Her pups grow for more than twenty years. Then they have pups of their own.

But education is spreading. Great white sharks are not vicious. Their sharp teeth are tools, not weapons. Scientists know it is possible to share the ocean. A great white just wants to live in peace.

Diving with great white sharks helps scientists learn more about them.

Great white sharks have a reputation for being vicious. But they are shy.

FUN FACT
Great white sharks can't live in captivity.

SWIMMING WITH GREAT WHITES

People can dive with great white sharks. Divers need to be in a cage. This protects the people and the sharks. Sharks come up close. They explore the metal cage. Sometimes they bite the cage. Diving with sharks teaches people about protecting them.

BEYOND THE BOOK

After reading the book, it's time to think about what you learned. Try the following exercises to jumpstart your ideas.

THINK

THAT'S NEWS TO ME. A shark traveled 20,000 miles (32,000 km) between March 2013 and March 2014. That's farther than any other recorded shark. How might news sources be able to fill in more detail about this? What new information could you find in news articles? Where could you go to find those sources?

CREATE

SHARPEN YOUR RESEARCH SKILLS. Gill nets are dangerous for many animals. Where could you go in the library to find more information about the effects of gill nets on animal populations? Who could you talk to who might know more? Create a research plan. Write a paragraph about your next steps.

SHARE

WHAT'S YOUR OPINION? Some people believe great white sharks are man-eaters. Many different media sources show sharks like this. Do you agree or disagree with this position? Use evidence from the text to support your answer. Share your position and evidence with a friend. Does your friend agree with you?

GROW

REAL-LIFE RESEARCH. Great white sharks can't live in captivity. But there are still places you can go to find out more information about them. Think about what kinds of places you could visit to learn more about shark conservation. What other topics could you explore there?

RESEARCH NINJA

Visit **www.ninjaresearcher.com/0066** to learn how to take your research skills and book report writing to the next level!

RESEARCH

DIGITAL LITERACY TOOLS

SEARCH LIKE A PRO
Learn about how to use search engines to find useful websites.

FACT OR FAKE?
Discover how you can tell a trusted website from an untrustworthy resource.

TEXT DETECTIVE
Explore how to zero in on the information you need most.

SHOW YOUR WORK
Research responsibly—learn how to cite sources.

WRITE

GET TO THE POINT
Learn how to express your main ideas.

PLAN OF ATTACK
Learn prewriting exercises and create an outline.

DOWNLOADABLE REPORT FORMS

Further Resources

BOOKS

Donohue, Moira Rose. *Great White Sharks*. Scholastic, 2018.

Gordon, David George. *Explore a Shark*. Silver Dolphin Books, 2016.

Pettiford, Rebecca. *Great White Sharks*. Bellwether Media, 2017.

WEBSITES

Factsurfer.com gives you a safe, fun way to find more information.

1. Go to www.factsurfer.com.
2. Enter "Great White Sharks" into the search box and click 🔍.
3. Select your book cover to see a list of related websites.

Glossary

breaches: A shark breaches when it comes all the way out of the water. When the shark breaches, it creates a huge splash.

dorsal fin: A dorsal fin is the fin that is on the shark's back. The dorsal fin was the only part of the shark the person could see.

endothermic: An animal that is endothermic can control its body temperature. Great white sharks are endothermic, unlike most fish.

exploratory: Exploratory means to find out more about something. Sharks use exploratory bites because they are curious, not because they are mean.

gill nets: Gill nets are a type of net fishermen use to catch fish. Sharks get trapped in gill nets.

migration: Migration means traveling long distances for food or space. Scientists think sharks make a yearly migration to the middle of the Pacific Ocean.

prey: Prey is an animal that another animal eats. Seals are perfect prey for great white sharks.

roam: To roam means to move without a set destination. The shark might roam more than 1,000 miles (1,600 km).

territory: A territory is the area an animal lives in. Sharks have a large territory to swim in.

vulnerable: An animal is vulnerable when it is in danger of being hurt. Great white sharks are vulnerable because of fishing.

Index

babies, 10–12, 26
blood, 7, 8, 13, 24
body heat, 14
breaching, 7

climate change, 18

dorsal fin, 13, 19, 22

eating, 7–8, 12, 14, 20–21
eyes, 4, 20, 22

fishing, 24

hunting, 4–7, 20–21

jaws, 7, 22

living near people, 22–27

migration, 9, 10, 14, 16–21

oceans, 4, 8–9, 10, 16–18

prey, 4–8, 12, 20–21, 24

scientists, 24–27
seals, 4–7, 14, 20–21
size, 4, 10–12, 17, 24–25
smell, 4, 7, 8, 10

tails, 13, 17
teeth, 7, 13, 20, 22, 26

where great white sharks live, 4, 9, 10, 14, 16–21, 22

PHOTO CREDITS

The images in this book are reproduced through the courtesy of: wildestanimal/Shutterstock Images, front cover, pp. 4, 8–9; Ramon Carretero/Shutterstock Images, pp. 3, 13; VisionDive/Shutterstock Images, pp. 4–5, 10–11, 26; Sergey Uryadnikov/Shutterstock Images, pp. 6–7, 12, 19, 20–21; lindsay_imagery/iStockphoto, p. 8; Martin Prochazkacz/Shutterstock Images, pp. 14, 23; Erwin Niemand/Shutterstock Images, pp. 14–15; Derek Heasley/Shutterstock Images, pp. 16–17; Red Line Editorial, p. 18; Nicholas Floyd/Shutterstock Images, pp. 22–23; Fiona Ayerst/Shutterstock Images, pp. 24–25; Chipmunk131/Shutterstock Images, p. 25; Tomas Kotouc/Shutterstock Images, pp. 27, 30.

ABOUT THE AUTHOR

Martha London is a Minnesota-based writer. She grew up loving all animals.